Tangled Roots

Also by Brenda Eldridge and published by Ginninderra Press

Poetry
The Silver Cord
It's All Good
A Personal View
Facing Cancer
From My Garden
Best Heard & Seen
Scarves

Non-fiction
Down by the River
Tales From My Patagonia
It's Still Out There
There's a Rainbow Serpent In My Garden

Edited by Brenda Eldridge and published by Ginninderra Press
Brave Enough To Be a Poet
The Heart of Port Adelaide
Collecting Writers

Brenda Eldridge

Tangled Roots

Acknowledgements

Previously published poems appeared as follows:

Best Heard and Seen: Athena; Balance; Old Garden Gate; Seascape; Seagulls; Another Seagull Story; Moon Daisies

Facing Cancer: Doubt Dragon; Cancer; Race for Life; The Sound of Hope; Comfortable Silence; Dark Shadow; In Awe; Dungeon; Time Passing; Bereft; Aftermath; The Outer Edge

From My Garden: New Life; Family Reunion; Saucer of Milk; Windows to Eternity; Grotto; Beyond Words; Because I Can; Intimacy; Pausing on the Beach; Dolphins in the Mist; Pelicans 2; Jetty; Lavender Butterflies; Smell-prints

It's All Good: Lost Sight; Old and New; Bitter Sweet; Copper Top; Eastern Mystery; Escapees; Gracious Dip; Misty; Fire and Mist; Ice Chips; Mirror After Mirror; Birds on a Wire; Naked ladies; Tree of Life (as Aftermath); Tree of Knowledge

A Personal View: A Distant View; Turning Back the Clock; Three Masts in the Sunrise; Honeywood Drive; Oh! (as Star-spangled Cobweb); Fire and Mist; Windy Night; Rings of Fire; Moonlight Dreaming; Night-time Calling; Pelicans 1; Moving On

Scarves: Silver Threads; One Like the Rest; Pretty With Pink Roses; A Bentwood Hat Stand; Sky-blue and Green; The Country Woman; Sweet Peas

The Silver Cord: Life – a Gift; Grieve No More, It's All Right, Mark; Silver Cord; Tapestry of Sound; Music in the Park; Earthly Silk; Cheeky; Defiance; Veterans; Fragment in Time; Laughter; Dreaming on the Sand

Tamba: Stranded Crab

Tangled Roots
ISBN 978 1 74027 869 0
Copyright © text Brenda Eldridge 2014
Copyright © cover photo Stephen Matthews Ginninderra Press 2014

First published 2014
Reprinted 2022

GINNINDERRA PRESS
PO Box 3461 Port Adelaide SA 5015
www.ginninderrapress.com.au

Contents

Introduction	9
Life and Death	
Life – a Gift	15
Grieve No More	16
It's All Right, Mark (2001)	17
New Life	18
Family, Memories, Time	
Family Reunion	21
Silver Cord	22
A Distant View	23
Lost Sight	25
Turning Back the Clock	27
Old and New	29
Three Masts in the Sunrise	31
Silver Threads	33
One Like the Rest	34
Colours	
Pretty With Pink Roses	37
A Bentwood Hat Stand	38
Sky-blue and Green	39
The Country Woman	40
Gemstones	41
Sounds	
Honeywood Drive	45
Bitter Sweet	46
Tapestry of Sound	48
Music in the Park	49
Earthly Silk	50

Characters

Cheeky	53
Copper Top	54
Eastern Mystery	55
Defiance	56
Veterans	57

Phenomena, Observations

Athena	61
Oh!	62
Escapees	63
Balance	64
Saucer of Milk	65
Gracious Dip	66
Misty	67
Fire and Mist	68
Fishing Without a Pole	69
Windows to Eternity	70
Fragment in Time	71
Old Garden Gate	72
Windy Night	73
Coorong Dreaming	74

Water

Ice Chips	77
Laughter	78
Seascape	80
Rings of Fire	81
Moonlight Dreaming	82
Grotto	83
Dreaming on the Sand	84
Beyond Words	85
Because I Can	86

Intimacy	87
Pausing on the Beach	88

Birds and Animals

Night-time Calling	91
Dolphins in the Mist	92
Stranded Crab	93
Mirror After Mirror	94
Birds on a Wire	95
Seagulls	96
Another Seagull Story	97
Pelicans 1	98
Pelicans 2	99
Jetty	100
Ovine Wine	101

Gardens, Flowers, Growth

Sweet Peas	105
Lavender Butterflies	106
Naked Ladies	107
Tree of Life	108
Smell-prints	110
Moon Daisies	111
Tree of Knowledge	112

Emotions, Trials and Beyond

Doubt Dragon	115
Cancer	117
Race For Life	119
The Sound of Hope	121
Comfortable Silence	122
Dark Shadow	123
In Awe	124
Dungeon	125

Time Passing	126
Bereft	127
Aftermath	129
The Outer Edge	130
A Year On	131
Moving On	133
Two Old Ducks	134

Introduction

When Stephen asked if I would like a 'new and selected' volume of my poetry to celebrate my sixty-fifth birthday, I was immensely pleased. He intended asking Jude Aquilina if she would be the editor. Gosh! Heady stuff indeed, especially when Jude agreed. Then the doubts set in. I thought, it will just be the same old poems; I'm trying to move forward; I don't want to keep looking over my shoulder to where I've been.

But I had two surprises in store for me. The first was the selection that Jude made from the seven volumes of my published poetry and some new poems I had sent her. When I went through her choices, I was astonished to hear the voice of a balanced and courageous person. All that writing to make things real and to clarify to myself how I wanted to be in the world had worked, but I hadn't realised how well.

My first collection, *The Silver Cord*, contained just a fraction of the hundreds of poems I had written when I chose to live not die. My heart, mind and spirit had been badly damaged by violence and broken dreams. Then, in 1991, one of my four sons took his own life. Three or four years later, not knowing how I could live with no dreams and the weight of guilt and grief, I went out one afternoon to end it all by driving off a winding mountain road to the valley far below. I couldn't do it. The call of life itself was too strong. So I set out to find out why I wanted to live and, more importantly, how I was going to do that in the future.

Since my childhood, I have had an image of being a dandelion – face upturned to the sun and filled with the joy of being alive. That dandelions are notoriously difficult to eradicate as they have a very tenacious taproot had not consciously registered in my mind at all, but here was evidence that my intuitive imagery was symbolic.

I turned to Mother Nature and found constancy. Through the changes of seasons, phases of the moon, regardless of the thoughtlessness of mankind, Mother Nature would eventually balance herself and new life would appear. That knowledge sustained me. No matter how far down I went, I could always come back up.

I learned we cannot always control what touches our lives but we do all have the gift of choice. We can choose how we are going to allow ourselves to be affected. Even no decision is a decision. I found that, if we're not vigilant, bitterness seeps in unnoticed and sours everything we do, think and say. I promised myself I would not become bitter and twisted. I learned that grief, anger and fear isolate us and that joy unites us.

My second collection, *It's All Good*, was a mix of old poems not included in *The Silver Cord* and some new ones written after Stephen first came into my life late in 2008. It had taken my youngest son ten years of constantly reminding me that it's all good – 'it' meaning life – before I accepted the wisdom of his words. It really is all down to how you look at it. I learned to look for the positives in everything and they are always there if you look hard enough.

As I write this, Stephen and I have been together five years. My poetry collections – *A Personal View*, *Facing Cancer*, *Best Heard and Seen*, *From My Garden* and *Scarves* – are like an ongoing journal. They cover retiring from a career in DSS/Centrelink spanning twenty-five years, my perspective of Stephen's run-in with cancer, and simple musings over everyday life. They also reflect how a constant and peaceful love does so much to heal old wounds.

I received the second surprise recently in the form of a letter from a friend and fellow Ginninderra Press poet. I had sent her a copy of my latest non-fiction book, *There's a Rainbow Serpent in My Garden*, about our trip to the Northern Territory and the amazing spiritual experience I had there at the end of 2013. I quote: 'Your book is, in a sense, cathartic, because I get a very strong feeling that you are more at peace with yourself than you have ever been…'

Yes, I do now have a different sense of myself. I am no longer fighting for survival, and I do have the right to be here. With the gods guiding me and with the support of beloved family and friends, I have come through. With Stephen, I have flourished. No longer a dandelion with a single taproot, I am a tree with a very complex root system. That is why this collection is called *Tangled Roots*, an idea illustrated so well in the cover photograph which Stephen took in Kakadu.

Everyone has a story – none more important or interesting than another. Sometimes it takes a shock like the death of someone dear to us to make us see that we are writing our own eulogy by the way we live our lives. We can influence how we want to be remembered.

I have been blessed with a brave heart and the gift of words, which has enabled me to know and understand myself. I hope my poetry will trigger positive thoughts within those who read it, so they too can feel more confident and assured of their own place in the world. Or better still, feel encouraged to pick up a pen and paper and explore what is in their own hearts and minds.

Life and Death

Life – a Gift

Life, relentlessly you pull and tug
And once, like a mindless marionette, I danced
Blissfully unaware of the magnificence of your gift
Carelessly drifting securely through childhood
Encapsulated, nurtured endlessly by my parents' devotion

I flaunted you with the blithe arrogance of youth
Surrendering in unresisting, gay abandon, as you beckoned
Blindly denying the existence of cruelty
Till you savaged my soul with uncompromising brutality
And I must lay my son in the embrace of the earth

Driven by despair, I wanted to leave you too
Yet in the eyes of my beloved you shone pure
Unable to go, I fought to want to stay with you
Your bounty was spread all about me
A splendid, panoramic wonder

I discovered your constancy everywhere
I didn't know till then you and loving were the same
An inherent sense of joy makes me laugh deliciously
Others are overcome by the urge to join in
In unity we dispel the gloom

Grieve No More

Grieving mother
Let me go
I need to fly
Don't hold me
Down here

Feet shackled
To the floor
By your demands
I loved him
He was of me

Let me love him
My way
Not conventionally
But freely
Openly

Let me love him now
As I couldn't
When he was alive
I don't want him
To be dead

It's All Right, Mark (2001)

24.12.69–5.4.91

I know you told me ten years ago
'It's all right, mum'
And your gift has held me safe
With some degree of sanity
Throughout the passing of time

As I struggled one morning
And found the words that simply stated
I don't want you to be dead
So this morning the words found me
'It's all right, Mark'

Grief has so many different faces
I have wept for you
I have wept for myself
Now I see I have been weeping
For us all

New Life

for Blaine Connor Hammond born 1 May 2009

Who is this person
Who has come into our lives?
Down's syndrome has marked him
He will not be a bright spark
His will be a special light
He will be a gentle glow
That will be untouched
By the storms of the big world
And no one will expect too much of him
Some will welcome his open affection
Many millions fought and died
So a child such as this
Can have a place to live his life
And be one who teaches us
When we get too clever

Family, Memories, Time

Family Reunion

It has been said
The reward for patience is patience
And I know this to be so
Long hours   days   nights   years
All have passed to bring me here

Grey clouds low and heavy
Are blocking the vision of the rising Sun
From my eyes
Though the increasing light
Proclaims his glorious presence

High overhead the waning Moon
Is softly glowing
Ever changing as she teaches
The ebb and flow – the dark and light of life
To those who wish to learn

This morning Venus too pulses brightly
Beautiful as always
Last to be seen in the dawn sky
She has been joined by her travelling sisters
Jupiter   Mercury   Mars

And I am once again humbled
By the vastness
Of this Universe
Knowing this too is only a speck
Of something much greater

Silver Cord

The clatter of hobnailed boots on cobblestones
Announced my paternal grandfather's arrival
Home from his allotment, brandishing a bunch of turnips
With all the aplomb of a royal gardener
Exhibiting his prize-winning, exotic, hybrid roses

My dad gifted my mother the bounty of the countryside
Posies of early bluebells and cowslips, a hat full of mushrooms
Baskets of apples and cherries to preserve
Armloads of logs for cheerful, winter fires
Swathes of berry-laden holly, ivy and mistletoe

Born midway through the century, I was blessed with a brave heart
Which took me to the other side of the world
Where my sons now walk, strong and tall
As children, presenting me with wild flowers, seashells and dreams
As adults, the sweetest gift of all – continuity

I watch, wonder-filled, my eldest grandson,
Poised in contemplation, his stance is like my dad's
I see my mother in the smile of the youngest child
The line reaches through each passing generation
Linking us forever, by a silver cord

A Distant View

My mother lives alone in the dark of blindness
She has not ever left the country where she was born
And she is approaching her eighty-sixth birthday
Without ever seeing dolphins in the wild
Or brilliantly coloured parrots and the shy koala

I tried to share with her the closing of a day
As seen from our balcony overlooking the tidal reach
With the exquisite apricot and yellow sky
Being eased from view by the palest grey
Then the purest of blue growing deeper by the minute

Did she see in her mind's eye the water
Turning to silver and grey ripples
The dancing reflections of orange and white
From the lights of the bridge
And the marina on the far side

Could she imagine the four dolphins
That cavorted in sensuous delight
Changing from silver to black silhouettes
The perfection of a passing pelican
She remembered from a child's ditty

I told her of the changing tides
The trickery of the wind on the surface of the water
The shipwrecks seen on the mud-flats
Listed the different birds that share this place
And all the while the young moon was lowering

In the listening I sensed a peace between us
Bridging the distance of half a planet
The passage of fourteen years between hugs
Strengthening the link that holds us together
Regardless of time, space and personality clashes

Lost Sight

For Mildred

Sight, I have at last accepted you are gone from me
Twenty years ago this battle started
When you began to slip away
Top surgeons fought valiantly again and again
But all they could do was postpone the inevitable

No more can I make that quick cup of tea
Before dashing to the shops on my bicycle
All those meals I made without thought
Now peeling and chopping vegetables takes so long
And I must concentrate when cooking a chop

How I miss watching people's faces
From their expressions, I learned far more than the words
I hadn't realised how much I lip-read
Now I am easily confused in a group
Trying to follow different conversations

I have become so dependent on others
Little things like telling me
I have spilled my tea down my blouse
Guiding me when I walk outside
So I don't step in something smelly

I've always liked to read in bed
Now I lie in the darkness
And listen to a beautifully modulated voice
Reading me the newspaper or a book
And I can always rewind it if I fall asleep

I listen differently now too
Notice inflections and accents
Wishing TV programs didn't have incidental music
It's hard enough to create the scenes
Without this added distraction

My mind, of necessity, has become singular
The quickness that could recall general knowledge
Now must be used to remember where I put things
It takes so long to find them
When someone thoughtlessly moves them without telling me

I can still remember so much though
A little slower perhaps, but the memories are there
Clear and unspoiled by time and age
Husband, children, grandchildren
Nature, neighbours, life in all its glorious abundance

Turning Back the Clock

Pale-faced children with enormous eyes
Too exhausted by hours and hours
Of terror and hard work
To notice the world around them
Or to question their reality

Parents deliberately kept ignorant
By schooling only being made available
To a privileged few
Surely the hearts of some parents
Must have been wrung at their children's plight

The cries for a better world were eventually heard
By those with enough influence
To bring about change
Taking the children out of the mines and factories
And putting them into classrooms

Eyes now shone with eager intelligence
They were hungry to improve their world
Make it a better place
For their grandparents, parents
And their own future children

History books can tell us how we came to this place
Where too many parents today
Are as blinded by affluenza
As our ancestors were by ignorance
Only now they are too lazy to care

Not wanting to see that we have come full circle
And we are sending our children
With the help of computers and electronic games
To a stultifying virtual reality
And they do not look up, around or ahead

Old and New

Comfortably old
Shabby cobwebbed
Timeless hotel
Ornate balcony railings
Overlooking the ocean

Fireplace stands
Polished empty
Reminder of another age
Television fridge
Keep it wedged in today

Clopping horses' hooves
Rumbling wagon and dray
Drowned out long since
By passing years
Never-ending cars

Would Renoir
Have cringed
To see copies
Of his artwork
Hanging on the walls?

Or laughed
At the eccentricities
Of a modern world
Seeking stability
From a precarious past

When knowledge
Was different
Uncluttered unverified by science
That has brought
Such wondrous freedoms

Three Masts in the Sunrise

We were walking to the train station
The sun hadn't been up long
The path through the Port Canal shops
Was decidedly ho-hum
As the working day launched itself

A few cars in the car park
People who appeared half asleep
Trudging heads bowed to the supermarket
With its bright lights beckoning
A biting wind tossing litter about

Three tall masts towered over the roof-tops
Rigging, to my uneducated eyes
Looking quite impressive
A row of pigeons sat comfortably
On the lines linking the masts

I was fooled for a while
Thinking it was a real ship
As I tried to remember
How there could possibly be
A stretch of water there behind the buildings

It was of course only a reminder of long-ago days
When real ships moored at the docks
Of a busy and thriving port
Where flags of many nations flew
On the forest of clanking masts

There would have been raised voices
Over the rattle and clip-clop
Of horse-drawn drays
On cobbled and paved streets
The shriek of the steam engine whistles

The mixed smells of horse dung
Hot tar sacks of grain
The tang of newly hewn timber
Bustling hotels adding the mouth-watering aroma
Of beer and roast meats

Amidst it all the clean smell of the sea
Unchanged since time began
Surging tides running up the river
Carrying the mournful cries of seagulls
And lost sailors

Silver Threads

At Christmas we used
To decorate our tree
With long strands
Of silver amongst
The coloured glass balls

We tried to pack it away
Carefully for the next year
But it always knotted
And looked scruffy
So new had to be bought

I was reminded of this
The other day
When I saw a
Single strand of silver
On the bathroom floor

Not a hair from my head
Rather a stray
From the scarf
I had been wearing
To warm my neck

There is something opulent
About silver threads
Shining in an otherwise
Plain and serviceable
Square of soft wool

One Like the Rest

Going to high school
Such a big change
Money had to be found
For a uniform of
Green and grey

The green blouses new
A dark green tie
A forest-green tricorn hat
Even the grey blazer was new
And the sports clothes

But my skirt was second-hand
And nothing like the other girls
With their neat grey knife pleats
And I knitted my grey jumper
No money to buy one from M & S

But I remember the joy
At being able to buy
A second-hand, machine-made scarf
Long, striped in greens and white
My badge of acceptance

Colours

Pretty With Pink Roses

How I loved my first scarf
None of that square
To be worn in a triangle
Covering hair, a shield from
Wind and rain, worn by old ladies

This was long and narrow
Only cheap polyester
But it was so fine
As I ran it through my fingers
Or tied with a knot to the side of my throat

I loved how it flew up
In the wind
So delicate the pink roses
Soft green/grey leaves
On a pale pink background

My mother used to talk
Of silk cloth so fine
You could thread it through
A wedding ring
Not silk, but my scarf could do this

Suddenly I had confidence
I became 'The eccentric
Englishwoman living overseas'
Ah, such unexpected freedom
With my new identity

A Bentwood Hat Stand

Lots of homes have them
Usually just inside the front door
Some are modern and metallic
Mine was of bentwood
And no place for hats or coats

As my collection of scarves grew
I displayed them on the stand
I tried to carefully arrange them
By their colours
Much like collected buttons

But the tidiness didn't last long
They quickly became a jumble
A riotous array of birds' wings
Depending on the mood I was in
What colour I wore each day

Never the same one
Two days running
How could I wear red
When my heart was lilac
Or gold like autumn leaves?

Sky-blue and Green

My lady is aloof
As she walks in the
Late spring sunshine
The roses only buds still
Forget-me-nots shy at her feet

Her gown moves like a bell
Around her slender body
Rustling softly as only silk can
Her picture hat threaded around the crown
With a long scarf

She pauses to look up into a tree
A bird is singing sweetly
But can she see it among the pale leaves?
The colours of blue sky and green
Are the same as her trailing scarf

The Country Woman

People have long teased me
About being a witch
I've been happy to go along
With the fantasy
Because I knew I wasn't

But I found exquisite joy
In wearing a green pashmina
I felt I was wrapped
In the green of the forest
Where nothing would harm me

I experienced instant changes
My whole being slowed down
I could put it over my head
And feel its warmth around my face
The call of the country woman so strong

No matter how busy
Everyone was around me
I was in my own private sanctuary
Surrounded by the calming influence
Of a green pashmina

Gemstones

The autumn midday sun
Shone brightly
While still leaving
The hazy mellowness
That lingers on the senses

Grapevines marched
Beside the road
Acres of living gemstones
Emeralds   rubies   topaz
Beneath a pale sapphire sky

Sounds

Honeywood Drive

Here I sit in front of a log fire
Not quite like the one from childhood
This is a square, glass-fronted pot-belly
But the embers glow with the same heat
The same magical pull to a fantasy world

In the kitchen quiet male voices
Exchange thoughts, a steady rumble
Nothing sharp or discordant
An interesting juxtaposition
Of American and English here in Tasmania

Layla the dog sleeps in her bed
At the top of the stairs
Like her master she is easy going
And neither of them miss much
Except the rabbits in the garden

Outside the winter rain is pattering on the roof
From the window I can look out
Over a stretch of water
A long watery arm of the sea
To a green hillside dotted with a few houses

How timeless this space
A timber-lined house
Uncluttered and gracious
Permeated by a sense of peace
Insulated from a busy world

Bitter Sweet

for Bill Evans

The crooners, the jazz singers
The country and western balladeers
All the musicians over time
Know how to do it

They reach within and deftly
Take the deepest feelings
And craft them into music and lyrics

They explore each wave of emotion
Acknowledge it, give it credence
Value it as a treasure
Then polish it till it shines
As pure as sunlight
Reflected on the water

They do not sing or play
For their audience
They weep and keen for themselves
For the joys and lost loves
The agonies of living life
That they feel with the same intensity
As any poet

The poet's words fall into silence
Hang like a dewdrop on a leaf
And eventually fall quietly to the earth
Forgotten for the most part

The singer, the player
Can perform their creations
And countless people will connect
Feel the blessed relief
That they are not alone
Someone else has felt pain
And given the listener the opportunity
To know themselves better

Tapestry of Sound

Strings blend harmonies
That take the spirit
In a flight
Soaring sweeping
Carelessly cascading

Drifting feather-like
Caught momentarily suspended
To roll like thunder
Ricocheting around the mountain tops
Reverberating in deep caverns

Plucking melodies
From the wind
Whispering, haunting
Weaving a tapestry of sound
With rainbow threads

Then airy as mist
Disappearing into nothing
Leaving only an echo
Gathering in the ether
To pour again

Music in the Park

Late afternoon, in the heart of the city
The parklands lay dozing
Under an autumn sun
The air was fresh and still warm
The earth richly damp from long-awaited rain

The trees were dull green
With the tired look they wear
Just before cold nights
Turn them to a blaze of
Orange and yellow fire

The sky was clear blue and dotted
With picture book puffy clouds
Sitting alone, cross-legged on the grassy bank
A young man played his violin
There was no one close enough to hear except the ducks

Earthly Silk

Grasses, reeds
Swishing softly
Bending before the wind
Single emerald strokes
Of brilliance

The earth like a swath of silk
Grasped by unseen hands
Lifted, draped
Like sheets on a bed
Billowing, settling

Shimmering with every breeze
Hillsides rippling
Mobile, fluid
Changing with each moment
Never still

Symphony of movement
Earthbound flight
Seed heads rattling
Whispering, sighing
Percussion in nature's orchestra

Characters

Cheeky

As I took my customary stroll
Along the river path to the bus stop
The sun was already hot at seven in the morning
My usual reverie was interrupted
By the soft tinkle of a bicycle bell

Hastily stepping to the side
I only glanced at the cyclist
Who sped past, crouched low over his racer
Not for him careful protection from the sun
He wore only a G-string, helmet and sneakers

His long slim back was beautifully tanned
And gleaming with perspiration
His cheeks sported the same all-over tan
Each one cleverly tattooed
With what looked, at too brief a view, like a rose

Copper Top

Onto the green she marched
Tanned legs taking long strides
Matronly navy-blue blouse and shorts
At odds with her young body
The dog trotted on ahead

The sun caught the copper
In her tightly drawn ponytail
My fingers itched
To release her fiery tresses
And destroy her prim tidiness

Images flashed of her dressed
In traditional Celtic costume
Straight-backed, light-footed
Cheeks flushed, eyes bright
Hair flaming like a halo

Eastern Mystery

She stepped out of her car
In a swirl of mauve silk
At first I thought it was a sari
Then I saw her origins were more Arabic
With her head and shoulders swathed

She carried with her
The very essence of Eastern mystery
Her voluptuous body
Wrapped in purple splendour
Full of hidden promise

Not like her Western counterparts
Flaunting partially anorexic bodies
Carefully tanned and pampered
Casual clothes revealing too much
Faces harsh and closed

Defiance

Close-cropped blonde hair
On a head held high
Her face was a turmoil
Of pensive defiance and misery
Daring anyone to pity her

With painstaking care
She crossed the road
Amid the midday traffic
Willing the lights not to change

The empty leg of her trousers
Proclaimed the inevitability
Of her shiny new crutches
Growing in familiarity
Then becoming the missing limb

Veterans

Our eyes met
I looked away
Caught by that open
Welcoming smile
I looked again

I recognised her
And wondered
What she had seen
In my face
Hers was so full of joy

She was different
More than extra weight
Greying hair
A quiet surety
'I have come through'

We stood on the causeway
Halfway between two land masses
Both walking alone
Self-appointed therapy
To heal the sorrows of our lives

Our histories similar
Married young, offspring
Trying to please our husbands
Both being battered and beaten
Yet unquashed

Tragedy striking us
Through our children
Now strong enough
To take back our lives
To go on creatively

Like battle-scarred veterans
Our wars made us weak yet stronger
Now we spar with the memories
Walk alone
And write poetry

Phenomena, Observations

Athena

Not the Greek goddess
But she arrived
This morning
With regal grace and dignity
Befitting royalty

A huge ocean liner
Gleaming white
Against a clear blue sky
And the deep waters
Of Outer Harbour

Two self-important tugs
Seemed to be
Herding her along
Like worrisome sheepdogs
With a skittish flock

But her progress was
Slow and steady
And for a moment
I wondered where she had come from
And where she was going

Oh!

The plane roared into life
Thundered down the runway
Took off like a heavy bird
And in the early morning darkness
Soared out over the ocean

To my surprise it did a U-turn
And as we flew back over the city
The sprawling network of streets
Lay like a star-spangled cobweb
Over the solid blackness of the earth

Escapees

They huddled in a tightly packed group
Beside the fountain on the mall
One broke lose and danced away
Then another and another
Till most of them were on the move

The tiniest breeze would send them off
Chasing each other in joy-filled abandon
I could almost hear them singing and giggling
One brave lot tumbled away
Determined to explore farther horizons

A few remained under the seat looking forlorn
Everyone was having a wonderful time
Who were these creatures of revelry?
Little white polystyrene shells
Used for packing parcels

Balance

Years ago I was out walking
Along a different river path
Surrounded by great gum trees
The grass thick and lush at their feet
Even the air seemed green

Sunlight twinkled and sparkled
Off the fast running water
As it leapt over rocks
And gathered swirling in pools
Before surging ever onward to the sea

Parrots were everywhere
Feasting on the gum blossoms
Keeping up a constant chatter
They knew how to live
Each day to the fullest

A fallen bloom shone brilliant red
Caught on a rainbow thread of cobweb
That stretched from one leaf
To another across the path
Its message was all about balance

Saucer of Milk

Beneath a pale blue sky
Studded with little puffs of cloud
The sea is like a saucer of milk
The horizon only visible by the presence
Of three enormous container ships

The early spring sun is just warm
On my head and shoulders
I cast a long shadow on the wet sand
The air is fresh and crisp
As I breathe in its peace

The tide is far out
And whispering seductive messages
As it rolls onto the sandy shore
With the delicacy of the lacy edges
Of a Sunday-best tablecloth

For once there are few people about
Just solitary souls walking their dogs
Or sending them dashing after a ball
Ah! A pelican has just cruised past
Wing tips so close to the smooth water

With the images of saucers of milk
Lace-edged tablecloths
Seaweed like scattered cake crumbs
How rich is this feasting table
I lovingly call my life

Gracious Dip

Before the dawn
Lightened the sky
When everything
Was hushed
Still sleeping

I slipped
From my bed
Padded
Barefoot
Through the house

Pausing by the
Open kitchen window
I leaned
Over the sink
Looked upward

Poised mid-dance
Sickle moon
Lying in a gracious dip
Morning star partner
Holding her by an invisible hand

Brilliantly
They gleamed
Shining in
The clear dark heavens
Stunningly beautiful

Misty

Sleeping hills
Silhouetted
Against a pearly sky
Clouds of softest pink
Feather delicately

Turning misty gold
As the sun climbs
Breaks free
Piercing the haze
With shafts of fire

Fire and Mist

The sun is newly risen
Sending long slanting rays
To reflect off the windows across the water
With more than white gold
It is like blinding shimmering fire

How quickly the sun is moving
Already the image has gone
Leaving the window a sheet of brightness
That hurts my eyes
But gives the building luminosity

Like an actor waiting at the back of the stage
The misty full moon is hovering
Serenely aloof
All night she has been the focus
Of attention in a cloudless sky

Fishing Without a Pole

With an invisible thread
Venus cast her line
Hooked the moon
And gently reeled her up
To arc across our daylight sky

Windows to Eternity

A poet paints with words
What the artist sees
And the worshipper adores
Knowing it is but a humble endeavour
That aches the heart of the writer

Perfectly reflected in the still water
The sun newly risen
Blinds the eyes with glaring brilliance
Swifts skim the surface
Mirrored images of flight

Infinitesimal movement
And light sparks like fire
There are two reflected suns
Moments pass and now there are three
Four   five   windows to eternity

Fragment in Time

On an autumn afternoon
Tall trees reach
Tired arms overhead
To make a tunnel
Of the narrow street

Regal parade
Still, timeless
Silent sentinels
Guard of honour
Casting deep shadows

Eyes drawn irresistibly
Along a pathway
Of soft dappled light
To an archway
Of blazing purity

White silver gold
Dazzling shimmering
Breathtaking spellbinding
Beckoning 'come hither'
With all the enticement of a lover

Old Garden Gate

Somewhere hidden in the foliage
A blackbird sung
Filling the quiet stillness
With golden notes
And joyous trills

A seat waited patiently
For someone to pause
To soak up the serenity of the garden
Or perhaps read a book
Or write a letter

The old wooden gate
Worn and storm-damaged
Held the key to mysteries
For those coming in or out
A puzzle – as there was no fence

Windy Night

Six months ago on the night we moved
Into this wonderful house beside the tidal reach
The wind through the mesh of the screen door
Sounded like a swarm of angry bees
And we woke the next morning
To see the water lapping over the stones
That keep the river safely off the footpath
And out of our garden

Tonight the wind has howled relentlessly
Varying from sounding like thunder
To a soft whine as it again
Tries to find its way inside our bedroom

We laughed at the idiocy of it
We exchanged images
You thought it sounded like
Someone trying to play the trumpet
I could imagine a large and blurry
Old-fashioned golliwog
Till I was reminded of the creaking
Of the London Underground trains

When I went into the studio
To get pen and paper
I glanced out across the reach
To see the new moon
Lying on her back
A picture of tranquillity
And the wind continued to howl

Coorong Dreaming

We had driven for miles
Then walked across
Pristine white sand dunes
Finding no firm footing
On their soft surfaces

Our voices were silenced
By the pure forces of nature
Waves roaring onto the shore
Nothing gentle about them
So much energy and noise

The sunlight lay like
Sheets of burnished silver
Dazzling our eyes
Sending our senses soaring
To float with ethereal clouds

A flock of terns huddled
Close together on the wet sand
In perfect harmony
With their world of raw elements
And countless broken seashells

(The harsh reality was
We were not the only visitors
To venture into this place
But did the others have to leave
Their rubbish behind when they left?)

Water

Ice Chips

Roused from the deepest of sleeps
Induced by an anaesthetist's skills
The touch of ice chips on a parched mouth
Is the first step back to reality
That moist tongue can lick dry lips

A drop of water trickles painfully down the throat
The breath catches, falters, starts again
With a cross between a gasp and a sigh
A befuddled mind has a vague awareness
Does a mental check
Do I hurt anywhere, can I feel myself?
Before drifting back into sleep

Time passes, a voice reaches in calling my name
Again the bliss of ice chips
And a surprise, a warm damp cloth
Passes gently but surely over my face and hands
Perhaps waking is not so bad
I learn a new appreciation of water

Laughter

My spirit felt cheerless
Wishing it were evening.
Stretching before me a day
The eastern sky
Brightened regardless

Grey clouds trembled
On the horizon
White gold almost violently
Poured out fingers of light
The sun split in two

The ocean lay dull
Green waves rolled onto the shore
Gradually soothed my mind
Sun broke through
Whitecaps shone

Shed shoes and stockings like weights
Danced barefoot at water's edge
Tiny waves sparkled with sunlight
Arms opened wide rejoicing
A heart overflowing with gladness

Childlike senses rushing
Fleeing cares, the caring
Music raising awareness
Freedom flooding the mind
Laughter bubbles unbidden

Long silent prayer of thanksgiving
Hugs the joy close
Too precious this gift to share
Feels the glow like a flame
Too long dimmed

Snowy gull sat on the sand
A black petrel flew overhead
Over the water a heron glided
Peace soaked my being
Lasting all day

Seascape

I found the courage to leave the forest
I walked the road less travelled
And explored the oceans of emotion
Where I learned the constancy
Of the ebb and flow of the tides

I witnessed the play of sunlight on water
The fragility of spindrift as it flies high
I plunged in and experienced the
Wonder of relinquishing control
As I floated, gazing upward at a daytime moon

I was gifted solace in a calm sea
And the laughter of a carefree child
As waves tried to knock me off my feet
And swirled like liquid glass
Around legs that weary sometimes of walking

Rings of Fire

We often hear of the 'pebble in a pond' effect
And while the imagery is rich
My mind tends to be too literal
And as I watch the ripples widen
They do always bump into the edge of the pond itself

'Ginninderra' is an Aboriginal word
That very loosely translated means
Spreading little rays of light
And certainly out on the tidal reach
We have seen this in action many times

But there is another perception
A single spark of fire
That ignites others to form rings of tiny fires
That ripple and sparkle
Into the far reaches of the universe

Moonlight Dreaming

When Debussy wrote 'Claire de Lune'
And Beethoven his Moonlight Sonata
They might have done
Just as I am doing now
At 4.30 on a winter's morning

The sky is very slightly hazy
And the moon on the full
Flooding brightness through the bedroom window
Urging me to open the curtains
Revelling in the silence
An invitation I could not refuse

The tidal reach
Is shivering and dancing
Lights on the far shore
Not reflecting in their customary singleness
Rather spreading over the surface
Turning it to a sheet of rippling silver
The moonlight is making sparkles
Flashes of pure brilliance

All the scene needs for perfection
Is one of the dolphins
To leap in the ecstasy I feel
As I have seen them do in the sun
And the way I can only dream of doing

Grotto

To speak of grottos
Conjures up images
Of dappled green stillness
Wet rocks and cobwebs
A small waterfall

Shafts of sunlight
A reminder of the
Brightness of day
That balances
The mysteries of the dark

Birdsong and bees buzzing
The trickle and chuckle
Of water becoming bubbles
Floating away like prayers
To the ancient ones

Dreaming on the Sand

Autumn brings coolness
In the early morning
There are few people about
Seagulls diving for breakfast
Are good company

The ocean rushing to shore
Seems to be in a hurry
Casting up countless shells
Different shapes and sizes
Broken crab pieces

Solitary white rose
Thrown into the water
Returns on the next wave
Not rejected
Left dreaming on the sand

Beyond Words

I have seen the reach like this
Times past the counting
But each time I can only stop
And take in the clarity
The stillness and the peace

There are no words to describe
The vision of the water
Faint ripples appearing now and then
As cheeky cormorants
And cruising dolphins pass by

It's more than perfect reflections
It's something to do with hidden depths
The reaching into the eternity of the universe
Which is still an illusion as there
Probably is an edge to it somewhere

Because I Can

Mother used to say
'Don't do something just because you can'
But this morning I have played
In the ocean for the first time this spring
Just because I can

The water for all its changing moods
Is constant
A living moving energy
Smooth and incredibly soft
As it embraces me

It tries to knock me off my feet
And I am able to laugh out loud
The child within still feels safe
A security that has nothing to do
With my shaky ability to swim

Standing on the shore, hair dripping
Water running down my body and legs
The wind cutting through my clothes
The sun is shining but not very warm yet
This has been another promise kept

Intimacy

Overnight rain has left
A glistening sheen of water
On the top of the balcony railing
The wood slats beneath my bare feet
Are cool and damp, making my toes curl

The round glass-topped table
Is beaded with moisture
As are the chairs
So there is nowhere to sit
And soak up the morning

Heavy clouds have gifted
An intimacy that a clear sky cannot
The tidal reach is still
Except for the circles and waves
Made by four dolphins

A small tussle within
I don't want to lift this scene
With a pen and words
Onto a piece of paper
But I don't seem to be able to help myself

Pausing on the Beach

If I stand at the water's edge
The waves lapping around my ankles
Are so cold it makes my feet hurt
Further along the dog-walkers are gathering
So my time alone is limited

When I look down the light is making
Liquid patterns that make me want to dance
The sun shining on the wet sand is blinding
And all the while the soft ebb and flow
Of the tide is gaining momentum

It is the constancy of the
Pale and waning moon
High above in a sky of fragile blue
That gives me a sense of balance
A restful equilibrium

Birds and Animals

Night-time Calling

Your soft 'huff' calls me from sleep
I hear the gentle swish of the water
As you circle and dive
I cannot resist the temptation
To get out of bed and go out on the balcony

The lights on the other side of the reach
Are stretching long fingers
Of silver and orange across the surface
But your movements send ripples
Far and wide that catch the reflections

I am filled with quiet joy
How I love these times
When the world here is hushed
And I am honoured to share
The nights magic with you

Dolphins in the Mist

There might have been those
Who thought there could be
Nothing new to write about
The early morning and dolphins
But they would have been wrong

Today the reach is shrouded in mist
Bringing with it a different silence
Wafting into patches of fragility
Like old net curtains being parted
Reminding me of English fog

In a clear moment
The still surface of the water
Was sliced open by the arcs
Of two dolphin fins
Gone again without even a splash

Then the solitary pelican appeared
Like a graceful galleon
Searching for a lighthouse
And all the while the rowers' coach
Could be heard giving muffled instructions

Stranded Crab

Stranded? Who? Me?
Stranded? Never!
I'm waiting to get on with life
There'll be a wave along
Any minute now to carry me

How did I get here?
Well I was just paddling in the shallows
And a big wave
Caught me by surprise
Washed me up on the sand

Why didn't I turn around
And scuttle back into the water?
I was mesmerised by the sun
It looked different from here
But I feel a bit dried out now

Besides   I told you
I'm waiting for some help
What do you mean?
It's too late   I'm stranded
Couldn't you give me a hand?

Mirror After Mirror

Wherever the sun
Touched the ground
Overnight rain
Gifted a glistening
Sheen to the road

This shining path
Wound its way
Through the wetlands
Mirror after mirror
Lying perfectly still

Broken only
By waterbirds
Chugging across the surface
Leaving an
Arrowhead ripple

Birds on a Wire

I wonder what they think about
Perched up there on the telegraph wires
For they have as many different poses
As you would find among people
Standing about on a railway station

Portly pigeons, full of their own self-importance
With their subdued discreetly tailored suits
And the subtle colouring around the neck
Like the waistcoat or tie
Worn by an old-fashioned dandy or rake

The galahs sitting as close as possible
Rubbing themselves against each other
Like adoring young couples
Swallows and swifts darting about for food
Returning faithfully to their partners on the wire

There is no particular uniformity
At first they appear to all face in one direction
Then a rebel will come in and face the other way
There is even the occasional busker
To be found singing for his supper

Seagulls

You have been corrupted
By the wasteful ways of man
Who leave tasty foodstuffs
Like an open-air supermarket
For you to scavenge among

You squabble and fight viciously
With others in your flock
Showing little mercy for the injured
The only harmony to be found
Is in the purity of your white feathers

This is so much easier than soaring
Over the foaming sea
Gimlet eyes ever searching
For the flash of a silver fish that
Will need all your skills to catch

Yet when you venture out over the ocean
You are still the message of hope
For a lone sailor who fears
He is lost and may never
Reach the safe haven of land again

And when your wings majestically
Ride invisible thermals
Or hover almost motionless on a brisk breeze
Perfectly balanced and aligned
You are poetry in motion

Another Seagull Story

There have been many times
When I have shrunk away
From seagulls that have been
Fiercely arguing over some
Discarded food scraps

I have been frightened
By one grabbing a piece of my lunch
As I was putting it in my mouth
And by the strength in their wings
As they hovered too closely overhead

But today I saw a very different scene
When I watched from the bridge
A nest of scruffy dried grasses
Perched precariously on a post
In the middle of the river

Huddled in it were three very small baby gulls
And the parent birds fed them
With infinite gentleness
Before one flew off for more food
And the other settled protectively over them

Pelicans 1

It was just a way to help children remember
That I learned a little ditty
'The beak of a pelican holds more than his belly can'
And comical misfits has been the impression
I have been left with, if I thought about them at all

Only by watching them every day
Have I seen they are anything but that
Spanish galleons of old comes to mind now
When I see them alone or in a flock
Sailing gracefully on the reach

Unlike the parrots that streak past
Reminding me of Spitfires in formation
Pelicans are more like B52 bombers
Heavy and cumbersome as they take off
Then cruising with impossible dexterity

They fly over the water so low
Their wing tips almost touch the water
Then rise as if pulled by an invisible thread
And they soar with the finesse of eagles
To land on a post as lightly as a ballerina

No they are not comical misfits
But if you get close enough to them
They do have a gleam in their eyes
A sort of patient amused tolerance
At the fuss us folk make over things

Pelicans 2

I have often wondered
About the solitary pelican
Who seems to shun
The company of the others
Who grace this part of the reach

Unusually of late
It has been coming
Close to the bank
Immediately outside my studio
And I sense it looking at me

I knew it must have a message
And sure enough research tells me
Pelicans teach us about buoyancy in life
How to rest and relax in spite
Of life's heavy weight

No matter how deep we plunge
Into the waters of emotion
Though it is difficult to rise
The pelican shows us
We can always regain the surface

Jetty

At the far end of the jetty
Not another person in sight
A pair of Pacific gulls
Hovered, suspended by the wind
Deep in conversation

Diving into the green
Choppiness of the sea
They found a good breakfast
While I spotted a fragile feather
On the ever-moving surface

Beneath me the waves
Were slapping against the pylons
The whole structure seemed to be
Swaying slightly under the constant
Buffeting of the wind

Out to sea a small boat
Looked like it was racing
Before the gathering squall
Safe harbour beckoned to us both
As I set off home

Ovine Wine

Acres and acres
Of wires stretched taut
Between thousands of
Ramrod straight posts
Like crosses in a military graveyard

Gnarled and twisted trunks
Supporting a knot
Of savagely pruned vines
Waiting in the winter sunshine
For the pulse of new growth

Gently grazing
On the verdant grasses
Between the rows
Sheep
Such efficient mowers

Not only do they eat the grass
No doubt they leave behind
Natures own fertiliser
I wonder if anyone will pick that
When they savour the bouquet of the wine

Gardens, Flowers, Growth

Sweet Peas

Memories of long ago
When summers seemed to last forever
As every child's summers do
Growing sweet peas
Near the back door of the old farmhouse

After my dad had used
Hazel sticks for his
Runner beans and peas
I was allowed to have
What remained for my flowers

I used to get teased
Because even with the help
Of two sticks and a piece of string
My rows still ended up
Crooked and wild

My sweet peas grew bushy
Such delicate frilled and lacy blooms
Pink, white, mauve and crimson
Oh, and the perfume
Nothing could ever be as sweet

Lavender Butterflies

'Lavender blue dilly dilly
Lavender green…'
A nursery rhyme from long ago
When the only lavender I knew
Was from England

Its flowers were like stems of wheat
Not crisp and golden
But soft and quietly mauve
Picked and dried to lay in small bags
Among the sheets and underwear

Now I have French lavender
Flourishing in my garden
These flowers are like dark purple bees
And the deep mauve petals at the tips
Look like butterflies sunning themselves

Naked Ladies

The summer seems endless
With the oppressive heat
And so very little rain
Water restrictions mean the lawns are brown
And the earth baked hard as concrete

How is it then these ladies grew?
I watched in amazement as daily
Nine slender stems of pinky-brown
Pushed their way up from hidden bulbs
Reminding me of clever photography

The blooms stretched like sleeping children
Waking from an afternoon nap
All arms and yawning mouths
Their soft pink petals emitting
One of the most delicious perfumes of nature

Tree of Life

Without warning the monster came
Advancing through sheltered valleys
Racing up hillsides with uncompromising despatch
Striking horror and terror
In the heart of every living thing

Rain has since fallen
A heavenly rinse settling the ash
Cleansing trees, buildings, the earth
Leaving in stark relief
A trail of agonising destruction

Gum trees now stand stupefied
Honey and saffron bark shining pure
From bole to crown the marks of
Cruel black fingers of death
Clawing upward hungrily

Branches reaching skyward
In supplication, beseeching a salvation
That did not come
Their leaves hang brittle and dull
Yet not lifeless

Conifers wait patiently like soldiers in formation
Tall sticks of charcoal
No giant artist will utilise
To create scenes of wonder and delight
Only the indignity of being cut down and forgotten

The earth lay denuded of soft green grasses
No fragrant flowers gifted splashes of colour
But beneath the surface
Regeneration already stirs
Promise of life

Smell-prints

I was working in the garden
Repotting some herbs
And my hands became scented
With parsley and rue (the herb of grace)
Then the unusual basil-mint

Not to be outdone
Wormwood and thyme
Left their imprint
Mixed with the smell
Of rain and damp earth

But I had not finished
The rosemary too was touched
And lingered with the
Celery and cucumber for lunch
And the delicate aroma of my small pear

I unpacked a bag of oranges
And put them in a basket
It was their tangy smell
That led me to writing a poem
While drinking a cup of tea with a buttery biscuit

Moon Daisies

Some call you ox-eye daisy
Which to my ears
Does not do you justice
For there are no echoes

Of your mystical powers
Folk-lore tells me
Your golden centre
Like a miniature mirror
Turns constantly to the sun
As the day passes

I love to see you in moonlight
When grasses are turned to silver
Your snow-white petals gleam
And shining threads of a spider
Link fragile stems together

Tree of Knowledge

What a laughable misnomer!
You teased and tantalised
On the roadside signs
Drew me onward and onward
Down the bending road

I thought of Yggdrasil
Of Nordic mythology
I thought of Adam and Eve
And their Garden of Eden
Excitement grew

At last I found you
Tree of Knowledge
And you bequeathed to me
The heights of the
Flood waters over the years

I chuckled at my own greed
How foolish I was
How devastating when I imagined
Ten feet of raging water
Where I now stood

Emotions, Trials and Beyond

Doubt Dragon

You couldn't help yourself could you?
Saw a window of opportunity
And you were in like Flynn
And all credit to you
You did a grand job – for a while

But I am wise to your tactics
You forget I've tamed you before
The first time you were called
The Why Road and you nearly got me
Took me to the edge of sanity too

The second time you were called Guilt
You certainly made me fight hard
Quick as a flash if I felt
The warmth of a smile in heart or mind
You hammered me back down

I turned you into a poem
I even used the F word
When I told you to go to hell in a basket
I didn't need you any more
And you are published

You came as Grief
That was the hardest of all
You almost succeeded in grinding
My love of life to dust
You cast such a long shadow

And in that guise
You are often sneaking around
Catching me off guard
With a piece of music
Or a familiar voice or laugh

Do you like your new name?
I thought Doubt Dragon
Acknowledged well your ferocity
You haven't changed much
Still an insidious monster

I have different strength now
Not as passionate and defiant
I have patience and quietude
A depth of love and support
You can't come close to destroying

So go your hardest, Dragon
If you think I need reminding
That you will always be
The darkness that makes
The light so precious

Cancer

The woman, the lover, the poet
All are being undone by this word
It is the echoes of other people's experiences
That are making me unwilling to examine
What I really think and feel

Horror stories come thick and fast
Both of my grandfathers
And my own father
Died because of cancer
But I was too far away to be a witness

Many times I have heard
Of heroic battles to overcome cancer
With surgery, radiotherapy and chemotherapy
Till the spring of life is eventually broken
But who tells of the quality of life won?

Of the deep joy and satisfaction
Felt by a mother or father
As they live long enough
To watch their children grow
While grieving for what they will miss

Clever words and good ones
But still the poet is on the run
I dare you to say it out loud
What if they don't destroy it?
What if it comes back bigger and better?

I learned the hard way
There is no trading with death
Is trading with life any different?
Better to say 'fuck it'
And live each day to the fullest

Race For Life

We seem to be like athletes
With all that build-up to bring us
To the starting blocks
And now here we sit in a room
Just waiting for what comes next

We have no horror stories
About our experiences in the hospital
The staff without exception
Have treated us with kindness and respect
But never the less, the race is just starting

I don't remember anyone telling me
About this thing called
The race for life
I thought we plodded along
Enjoying the world around us

Making the best of every day
Trying not to hurt anyone
Jumping the occasional hurdles
Falling flat on our faces
Limping along at times

Even wondering vaguely
How long the journey would be
Being shocked to the core
When some lives were so short
Suddenly it's like being in a military unit

Where life is so much
'Hurry up…and wait'
'Prepare for the worst
And hope for the best'
We would rather be watching the dolphins

The Sound of Hope

Not for us the strains
Of perfectly harmonised notes
The soaring cadence of voices
Rejoicing in the joy of life
As written by a gifted composer

Or the sound of rain
Falling on a tin roof
Marking perhaps the beginning
Of the end of
Devastating drought

We listen intently
To the doppler
As it measures the strength
Of the blood flowing through
The veins after the bone graft

We hear that beautiful sound
And know a small release
Of the tension within
Yes the surgery is working
It is for us the sound of hope

Comfortable Silence

It has been a desire
For so many long years
To sit in comfortable silence
With one who is untroubled
By the lack of noise

We are trapped here in the hospital
Around us are the continuous
Background noises
Bangs and clatters of equipment
Sometimes a loud cry

In this room there is
The rushing sound of oxygen
A machine beeping
The soft rustle of a foot
Moving across the sheets

But we are at peace
He is reading a book
And resisting falling asleep
I sit here writing
It's like a river always flowing

We make our own haven
Wherever we are
Alert and attentive
To each other's needs
Nourished by this peace between us

Dark Shadow

What exquisite sensations
Through heart, body, mind and spirit
To know the trauma and indignities
Were not in vain
That the bone is clear of cancer

Still a rough road to be walked
The precautionary radiotherapy
Would like to threaten our peace
But you – the uninvited, unwelcome guest
No longer have the prime place in our lives

What a dark and terrifying shadow
You have cast
I have experienced fear in many ways
But nothing like you with your
Brooding presence waiting to pounce

Keeping us taught inside
As if we have been held together by
Over-stretched elastic and rusty paper clips
Daring ourselves to feel the joy
But always something held in reserve

We are not so arrogant
That we can cast care to the wind
No doubt your echoes will haunt us
But now you are just another name
For the darkness that makes the light so good

In Awe

The nurse calls his name
Her voice is warm
And full of caring
When she asks the inevitable
'How are you today?'

And he answers
In a strong voice
As he strides to meet her
That he is doing all right
This makes me weep

I am in awe
Of his courage and fortitude
His ability to be calm
When all I want to do
Is run and run and run

Dungeon

I don't know why
I can't seem to bring
The outdoors into
This dungeon of a
Waiting room

There are no windows
No breath of fresh air
The leaf-sprigged carpet
A mockery
Of a forest floor

The TV is never turned off
And even the cheerful staff
Can't change the fact
We are separate
From the other real world

Of sunshine and rain showers
Gleaming wet roads
The delicate call
Of birds in the trees
The hustle and bustle of life

Time Passing

It is not cowardice
That finds me in this garden
A place of seclusion
While Stephen has his treatment
In suite five today not suite two

How I despise the television
With the American voices
Whining and nasal
Stirring their mixing bowl
Of shallow dramas

But more disturbing
How sorrowful are they
Who sit attention glued to the screen
Can that really be better
Than their own reality?

I've vowed and boasted
I wouldn't wish time away
But it is hard these days
To stop thinking
'Let's get another treatment over'

I find a goal in each new week
Something to look forward to
Today there is only one more Wednesday
Tomorrow there are only
Single-number days to go

Bereft

Our lives have been caught up
With the hospital schedule
Living day to day
Varying our activities
Around the appointment times

I haven't given much thought
To whether the treatment is working
I don't lack courage
But it seems a pointless exercise
Speculating about the unknown

But soon we will be cast loose
Only two more treatments
Then we are on our own again
Without the ponderous presence
Of the hospital system

There is trepidation in my heart
I have become so used
To having our lives dictated to
By dietary needs, treatments
Keeping up a brave face

I don't feel so brave today
It has been a long journey
And I am bone weary
Of pretending to be all right
That my senses aren't being battered

Instead of rejoicing
I feel grief-stricken
In the weeks ahead
We must forge a new normal
Which will have some of the old

Aftermath

I wrote once about
The aftermath of a bushfire
And how the sweet blessing
Of rain falling cleansed
The earth for new growth

How well I know
The relief and healing
Of shuddering sobs
And tears that fall
As if without end

I hope there will be
No end to the tears
I have fought bitterness
Too hard for too long
To let it win now

Tears from the heart
Can only do good
It is sad that some
Seek only to stem the flow
Because they feel uncomfortable

The Outer Edge

I feel like someone has had me
At the end of a long rope
And it delighted them to
Swing the rope and me around
Like an Olympian twirling a hammer throw

All energy was concentrated
On establishing the right momentum
Calculating in the relevant forces
Making exacting demands for accuracy
Factoring in resources

It wasn't me anchored to the ground
I was too busy swirling
Desperately trying to identify familiar landmarks
Grasping onto those who beyond all logic
Gave me some semblance of steadiness

Now the unseen hand has set me free
No longer twirling and swirling
I have been granted a new perspective
Where the core of me is stronger
And the dross has been flung to the outer edge

A Year On

The all-clear result
Has lifted the weight of anxiety
And I find myself looking in wonder
At this man who has been
Through so much

Dear and observant friends
Have called him stoic and steady
And above all else he is that
But I witness the boy within
Laughing at the worlds seriousness

As we eat our lunch on the balcony
He feeds bread to the seagulls
He is full of delight and praise
For the ones who catch it on the wing
Demonstrating their awesome skill in flight

But he is contemptuous of the ones
Who sit on the ground
Squawking abuse at each other
Jealously guarding a patch of grass
While missing the offerings of food

But sadness fills my heart
When I see the network of faint lines
That have appeared at the corner of his mouth
Where he has learned to accommodate
The numbness, the price of life

I see the fleeting look of bewilderment
How can this have happened to me
But he sees people like seagulls
And chooses to encourage flight
Instead of sitting about complaining

Moving On

There are those among you
I have loved
And that love will enhance
All the rest of my days
With a sumptuous glow

There are others I respected
Yet no warmer feelings
Stirred in my heart
But respect is no mean feat
In a world gone mad on shallowness

Others I didn't like much at all
That constantly reminded me
We are all just people
Doing the best we can
With what we have each day

Who am I to pass judgement
I have been disliked
I have been respected
I have been disrespected
And I have been loved

Two Old Ducks

Romance isn't just for the young
Who at twenty-one think
They have all the answers
When they have barely begun
To be aware of the questions

The gods have been kind
To two people who have lived
Their gifts of life to the fullest
Daring to walk the roads
Less travelled by

Paths only intersecting
In the mellow autumn
Walking together hand in hand
With hearts still brave and strong
Finding joy in everything

Sometimes rather bewildered
By such good fortune
Mindful that love and hope
Are like romance –
Not just for the young

www.ingramcontent.com/pod-product-compliance
Lightning Source LLC
Chambersburg PA
CBHW070915080526
44589CB00013B/1305